D1481029

NOT JUST ANOTHER Christmas Book

9 Jazzy Piano Solos with Optional CD Accompaniments

Arranged by Mike Springer

Jazz music is fun to play year round, especially at Christmas time. From driving swing to jazz waltz, the *Not Just Another Christmas Book* series has it all. The carefully crafted arrangements are perfect for Christmas parties and recitals, or they can be used simply for fun.

Additionally, the books are truly unique because they contain accompanying CDs that feature bass and drum parts to create the sense of playing in a jazz trio. Each tune has three different CD tracks in the following order:

- For listening, the *Performance Model* track features the piano, bass, and drums in a complete performance.

- For practicing, a *Practice Tempo* track features the bass and drums (without the piano part) at a slow tempo.

- For performing, the *Performance Tempo* track features the bass and drums (without the piano part).

For practice and performance ease, a two-measure drum lead-in is given at the beginning of every CD track. Metronome marks for both tempos are given at the beginning of each arrangement.

Contents

For my mentor and friend, Dr. Jerry Wallace

Produced by
Alfred Music Publishing Co., Inc.
P.O. Box 10003
Van Nuys, CA 91410-0003
alfred.com

Printed in USA.

ISBN-10: 0-7390-8115-2
ISBN-13: 978-0-7390-8115-0

Cover photos
scizzors cutting paper: © istockphoto.com / hatman12 • ribbon: © istockphoto.com / egal • Christmas wrapping: © istockphoto.com / fotoAta

The First Noel

1 Performance Model
2 Practice Tempo (♩ = 63)
3 Performance Tempo (♩ = 84)

Traditional
Arr. Mike Springer

Santa Claus Is Coming to Town

4 Performance Model
5 Practice Tempo (♩ = 100)
6 Performance Tempo (♩ = 144)

Music by J. Fred Coots
Arr. Mike Springer

Jingle Bells

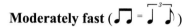
7 Performance Model
8 Practice Tempo (♩ = 112)
9 Performance Tempo (♩ = 144)

Words and Music by James Pierpont
Arr. Mike Springer

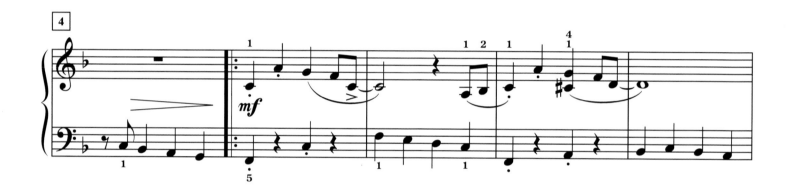

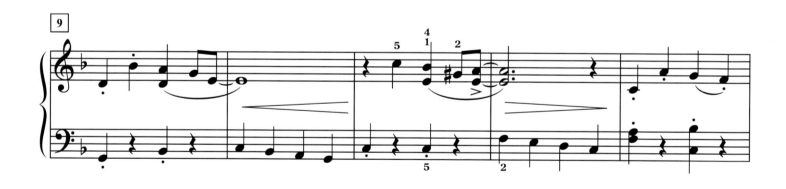

O Christmas Tree

10 Performance Model
11 Practice Tempo (♩ = 60)
12 Performance Tempo (♩ = 88)

Traditional
Arr. Mike Springer

It Came Upon a Midnight Clear

13 Performance Model
14 Practice Tempo (♩ = 100)
15 Performance Tempo (♩ = 120)

Traditional
Arr. Mike Springer

(There's No Place Like) Home for the Holidays

16 Performance Model
17 Practice Tempo (♩ = 100)
18 Performance Tempo (♩ = 132)

Words by Al Stillman
Music by Robert Allen
Arr. Mike Springer

O Little Town of Bethlehem

19 Performance Model
20 Practice Tempo (♩ = 80)
21 Performance Tempo (♩ = 100)

Music by Lewis H. Redner
Arr. Mike Springer

Silent Night

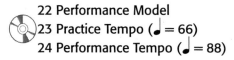
22 Performance Model
23 Practice Tempo (♩ = 66)
24 Performance Tempo (♩ = 88)

Music by Franz Gruber
Arr. Mike Springer

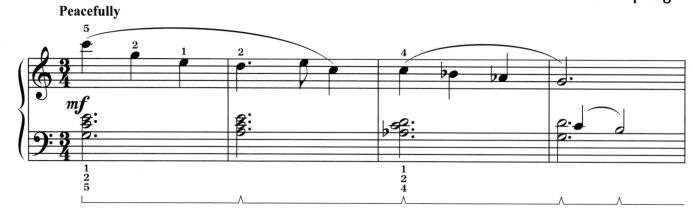

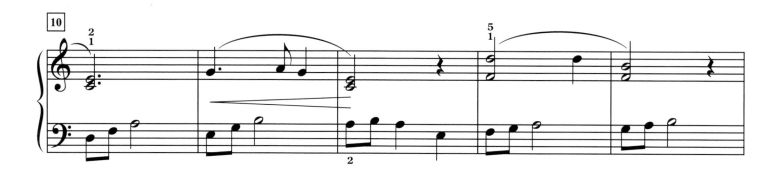

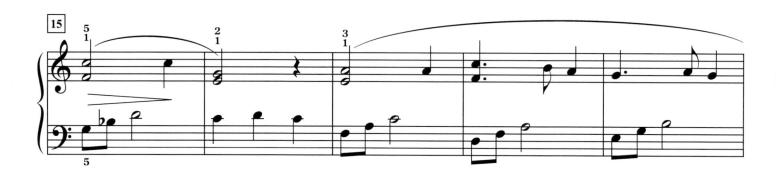

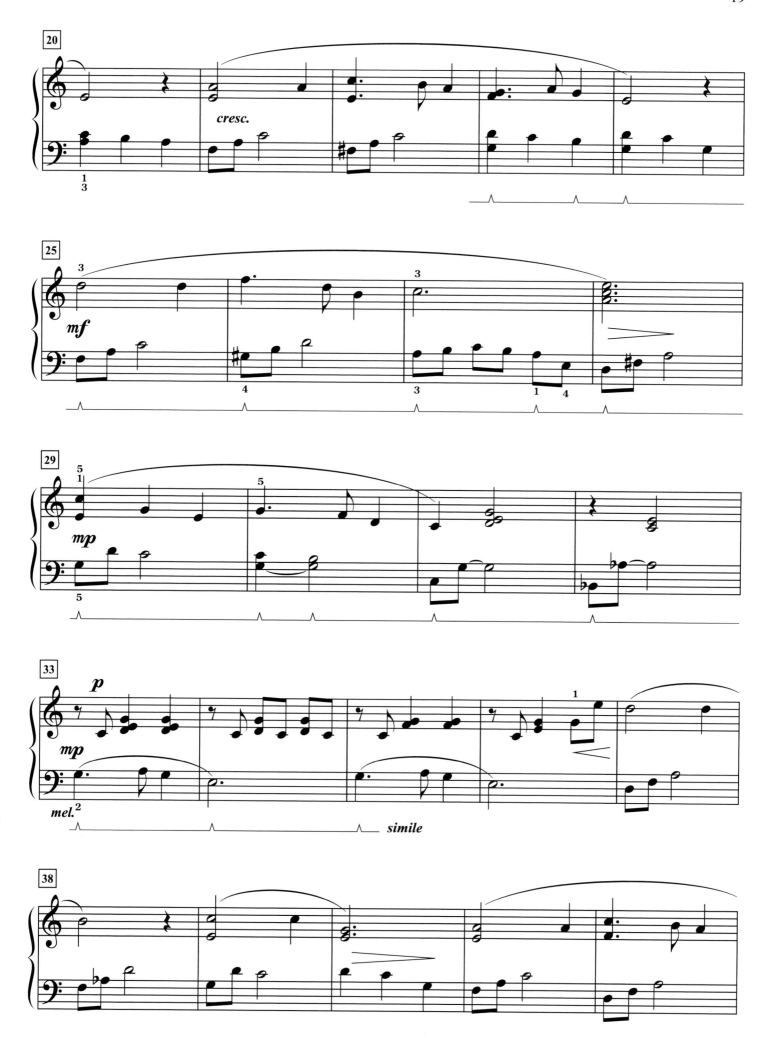

We Wish You a Merry Christmas

25 Performance Model
26 Practice Tempo (♩ = 100)
27 Performance Tempo (♩ = 144)

Traditional
Arr. Mike Springer